T0195594

THE ARMOR OF LIGHT

PROTECTION FROM SPIRITUAL DARKNESS

CHARLES A. NESS

WESTBOW
PRESS®
A DIVISION OF THOMAS NELSON
& ZONDERVAN

WestBow Press books may be ordered through booksellers or by contacting:

WestBow Press
A Division of Thomas Nelson & Zondervan
1663 Liberty Drive
Bloomington, IN 47403
www.westbowpress.com
1 (866) 928-1240

Because of the dynamic nature of the Internet, any web addresses or links contained in this book may have changed since publication and may no longer be valid. The views expressed in this work are solely those of the author and do not necessarily reflect the views of the publisher, and the publisher hereby disclaims any responsibility for them.

Any people depicted in stock imagery provided by Getty Images are models, and such images are being used for illustrative purposes only. Certain stock imagery © Getty Images.

Scriptures taken from the Holy Bible, New International Version®, NIV®. Copyright © 1973, 1978, 1984, 2011 by Biblica, Inc.™ Used by permission of Zondervan. All rights reserved worldwide. www.zondervan.com The "NIV" and "New International Version" are trademarks registered in the United States Patent and Trademark Office by Biblica, Inc.™

All italicized portions of scriptural quotations reflect emphasis added by the present author.

ISBN: 978-1-9736-2336-6 (sc)
ISBN: 978-1-9736-2337-3 (e)

Library of Congress Control Number: 2018903701

Print information available on the last page.

WestBow Press rev. date: 03/27/2018

Acknowledgements

My thanks to the Lord for his grace extended to me in the Lord Jesus Christ. I am thankful for godly heritage passed on to me by generations of faithful servants of the Lord. Thanks to my wife, Janet, and our family, who have been a great support in ministry; to Earl Falls and Beth Roth, who first challenged me to put on the armor of light, and for their valuable editing assistance; to Paula Marolewski, for her editing skills; and to Dr. Mike Spinelli, Pastor of Perkiomenville Mennonite Church, for his suggestions. Thanks also to the Perkiomenville Mennonite Church and the men in Bible study at the State Correctional Institution at Graterford, Pennsylvania, who first heard this teaching; and to all those who are applying this teaching in their lives.

CⲞNTENTS

INTRODUCTION

As I considered writing this book, I asked myself, "Why write another book on spiritual warfare?" You may be asking the same question. It would seem that everything has already been written on this topic. However, as I searched bookseller websites, I did not find one book written from this perspective.

I have been active in deliverance ministry and spiritual warfare for more than thirty years. I preached and taught on the subject. I read many books and attended seminars to better understand the dynamics of this topic. I thought I had a fairly complete knowledge of the scriptural teaching and practice of warfare ministry. I understood and practiced putting on the whole armor of God as listed in Ephesians 6.

Therefore, I was dismayed when a brother in Christ mentioned the need to put on the armor of light. I am embarrassed to say that I wasn't sure what he was talking about. He said, "Read Romans 13:12." I read it and was at a loss to explain what the armor of light is:

> The night is nearly over; the day is almost here. So let
> us put aside the deeds of darkness and put on the armor
> of light. (Romans 13:12)

This started a journey of learning that has been very exciting and revealing. I discovered truth I was unaware of, and this has led to a new way of praying, both for myself and for others. It has been an effective weapon in the battle against the devil and his influence.

As I was studying, there were doubts about the concept. I wondered about its validity and whether anyone else had experiences with the armor of light. When I read the introduction to *Jesus Calling*, by Sarah Young, I received confirmation as she described experiencing the covering of light and its effect in her counseling ministry (see chapter 8).

My prayer is that through this teaching, you will also learn new ways to effectively stand against evil forces and walk in new levels of victory.

CHAPTER I

THE NEED

The thief comes only to steal and kill and destroy; I have
come that they may have life, and have it to the full.
—*John 10:10*

Engaging in spiritual warfare presumes t there is, indeed, a battle. It presumes there are entities that are at war with each other. John 10:10 is the key to understanding the nature of that battle. Jesus makes it clear that there is an enemy of the believer. There is an entity, described in scripture in various ways and with numerous names, who is opposed to God's agenda for humans—and therefore to those who are followers of God. This being is generally referred to as Satan or the devil.

In the Beginning

Genesis describes how that conflict of the ages became part of the human race. When the serpent tempted the woman to eat the fruit of the forbidden tree and she ate it, the battle began. As a result, a curse came upon the world. This battle began at some point in the past in the heavenly realm. It is beyond the scope of this writing to delve into the origin of evil, but a study of Isaiah 14 and Ezekiel 28 may give some insights.

The record of holy history is a description of this battle. It describes God seeking to establish righteousness and Satan's intervention to block it. This evil is constantly progressing. When Adam and Eve ate the fruit, there was sin in the individual; when Cain killed his brother Abel, there was sin in the family; and later when Lamech bragged about killing several persons, there was sin in society. Sin got so bad that God sent the destroying flood. But it didn't stop there. Job's severe trial, the confrontation of Moses with the powers in Egypt, the idolatry of the nation of Israel, and those who tried to have Daniel killed are a few examples of this battle.

The battle continued and intensified with the coming of Christ. Throughout his earthly ministry, Jesus again and again confronted evil forces. Demons cried out for mercy, and religious leaders tried to stop his ministry out of fear that they would lose influence and power. Ultimately, Christ was nailed to the cross as the culmination of Satan's plan to defeat godly influence in the world.

Not only are humans caught up in this battle, but the earth itself is groaning to be delivered from the curse. One can only imagine what this world would be like if evil had not come upon the earth and the human race.

> For the creation waits in eager expectation for the children of God to be revealed. For the creation was subjected to frustration, not by its own choice, but by the will of the one who subjected it, in hope that the creation itself will be liberated from its bondage to decay and brought into the freedom and glory of the children of God.
>
> We know that the whole creation has been groaning as in the pains of childbirth right up to the present time. (Romans 8:19–22)

This warfare is both personal and corporate. In the personal realm, the enemy attacks individuals. We wage war against the world, the flesh, and the devil. This is the basic level of conflict, and it is a daily struggle. But the warfare is also corporate in that the devil works through social and political structures to achieve his goal of domination.

It is important to know and understand that this battle is not between two equal forces. God is the all-powerful Creator of all things, including the person we call the devil. As a created being, the devil is limited in all ways compared to God. Though he is a strong being with more power than humans, he has limitations. In addition, through the sinless life, death on the cross, resurrection, and ascension of Jesus Christ, Satan is defeated. He lost in his quest to defeat the Son of God and to conquer the world. The book of Revelation describes his ultimate destruction. Meanwhile, he is still trying to influence humanity and to obtain followers of his agenda. The good news is that, as believers in Christ, we have authority and victory over him.

CONTEMPORARY EXPERIENCE

While this is an ancient battle, it has taken a powerful turn in recent years. One can easily observe that there has been much change in our Western culture. The adversary has unleashed attacks on society that have resulted in significant changes in a number of areas:

- **The creative arts.** Music, TV, movies, the Internet, and other creative venues explore sinful, dark, and immoral topics.
- **The media.** There has been a measurable shift in the values and morality presented in the news.
- **The women's movement.** While making some needed corrections to the way women were treated, the movement has gone beyond historical social norms and biblical teachings about male and female relationships.
- **Abortion.** Eliminating children for "convenience" has become an acceptable form of child sacrifice.
- **False teaching.** The promotion of false Christs or an anti-Christ spirit is running rampant.
- **Sexuality and gender.** Sexual promiscuity including rape among adults and the sexual abuse of children. Homosexual relationships are encouraged, and the nature of gender itself is being called into question.
- **Youth.** Teen suicide, youth anarchy, and sexual laxity and perversion are common themes among young people today.

These are obviously not the only changes in our world, nor are they the only cause of the evil around us. As noted earlier, evil is always progressing. What one generation tolerates, the next will accept.

Some have expressed this tendency this way: "Evil is at first abhorred, then tolerated, and finally embraced." Another version says, "First evil is tolerated, then embraced, and then hailed as being good; then it becomes unlawful to do what is actually good."

This unleashing of evil has given new meaning to the words of Jesus in John 10:10 that the enemy comes only to steal, kill, and destroy. It is his intent to *steal the believers' peace, rob them of their joy in the Lord, and destroy their testimony.*

This renders believers ineffective and unproductive as ambassadors of the heavenly kingdom. There is no individual, church organization, community, or country not touched by this evil. Some think the devil seeks to physically kill believers, but an ineffective, defeated Christian is a more valuable tool to the enemy than a dead one. This is not to deny that there are many who have been martyred for the cause of Christ.

Other New Testament writers also describe this conflict in similar terms. The apostle Paul gives detailed instructions in 2 Corinthians 10 and in Ephesians 6 on how to prepare for this battle. Peter in chapters 4 and 5 of his first epistle warns of suffering for Christ and describes the enemy as prowling around like a lion ready to devour. The book of Revelation vividly depicts the conclusion of this battle.

Change is a constant in our world; that being said, change is not always from the adversary or from evil. Good and evil are determined by the motivation for the change, the nature of the change, and the direction that the change takes us. God says that he will shake things, and that will bring change:

> See to it that you do not refuse him who speaks. If they did not escape when they refused him who warned them on earth, how much less will we, if we turn away from him who warns us from heaven? At that time his voice shook the earth, but now he has promised, "Once more I will shake not only the earth but also the heavens" ...

Therefore, since we are receiving a kingdom that cannot be shaken, let us be thankful, and so worship God acceptably with reverence and awe, for our "God is a consuming fire." (Hebrews 12:25–26, 28–29)

THE SPIRIT FIRST

According to 1 Thessalonians 5:23, we, as humans, are made up of three parts: spirit, soul, and body. Genesis 1:27 states that humans are made in the image of God. God is a spirit, so therefore humans made in his image are also spirit beings. We are spirit beings with souls and bodies, not bodies with spirits.

The spirit is that part of us that is conscious of God. It is that part of us that will never die but live for eternity. Because we are born as sinners, our spirits are dead toward the things of God. When we repent of sin, confess Jesus Christ as Lord, and accept the provision of salvation, the Holy Spirit quickens our spirits, and we are born again. It is the spirit that sets us apart from the animal world. The spirit, as that part of us that will never die, represents the true person. We are first and foremost spiritual beings. We need to think of ourselves as spiritual beings and not just as physical beings.

The soul comprises the mind, emotions, and will. It is that part of us that makes decisions, and the soul is that through which we relate to those around us.

The body is the physical part of us that is visible, and through it we interact with the physical world.

Because of sin, we are born with the tendency to live from our souls and bodies. We do what satisfies the desires of our senses. The Bible refers to this as "the flesh." The flesh does not seek God and his righteousness; rather, it seeks to fulfill sensual desires.

It is God's will that we live from our spirits. We should live from our spirits out rather than from our bodies in. This is a fundamental understanding that is missing in much of Western Christianity. We are conditioned by our culture to think and act first from the body and soul. Therefore, many Christians are bound by habits and addictions and don't walk in the Spirit. We often yield to temptation because we act from our emotions (souls) rather than from our spirits. Decisions should be filtered through the spirit. The Holy Spirit quickened our spirits in conversion, so the Holy Spirit operating through our spirit informs the soul, which in turn influences what we do in our bodies.

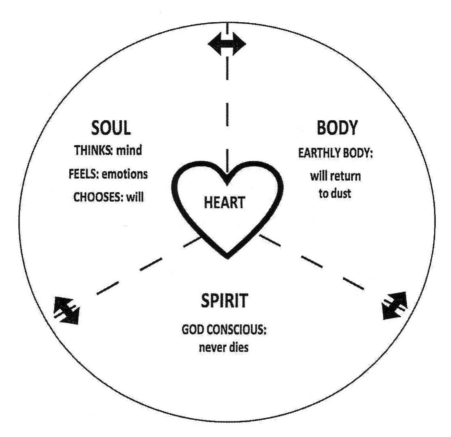

For us as Christians, every thought and act should be an act of worship. Such worship should flow from our spirits, which will then affect the rest of our lives and others.

Because we are spirit beings, that is where the enemy attacks. His goal is to make us spiritually ineffective. He will use the body and soul as a gateway to the spirit. The more a person gives in to the desires of the flesh, the more impotent he or she becomes spiritually.

The conflict we face is spiritual. That's why it is called "spiritual warfare." It is a battle not only between the spiritual forces of God and the devil; it is a battle for the human spirit. Therefore, we need protection for the spirit. The armor of light and other weapons described in scripture are not physical but spiritual in nature. They alone are effective for spiritual protection and victory.

This conflict of the ages that began far in the past will continue until that day when the devil and his angels are cast into the Lake of Fire. As humans, we are caught in this conflict. This conflict is real and affects everyone whether they realize it or not. For followers of Christ, it is a daily exercise of being on alert to the enemy's tactics and standing firm in our faith. It is the intent of this writing to provide a much-needed resource for victory.

It is also important to note that not all temptation to sin is an attack from the enemy. James 1:14 states that "each person is tempted when they are dragged away by their own evil desire and enticed." The devil cannot be blamed for sins that we commit in response to our sinful desires. There has been much misunderstanding about this, and as a result, some Christians have not taken responsibility for their sin. Instead, they consider temptation a spiritual attack. Some even go so far as to see temptation as demonic activity and seek deliverance from demons. While there is a time for deliverance ministry, not all sin is the result of demons. Many times, sin in a person's life is the result of the conflict between the spirit and the flesh within a person. As noted earlier, there are three enemies of the believer: the world, the flesh, and the devil. Spiritual armor is primarily a form of defense against the devil.

CHAPTER 2

ARMOR AND LIGHT

The night is nearly over; the day is almost here. So let us put aside the
deeds of darkness and put on the armor of light.
—*Romans 13:12*

Where is the armor of light? To understand, we need to answer two
other questions: what is armor? and what is light? These will be
explored from both a natural and spiritual perspective.

WHAT IS ARMOR?

Armor is a military term to describe what is worn as a defense against
an attack with weapons. In ancient times, soldiers wore suits of metal
to protect against being punctured by swords, spears, or arrows. They
carried shields and wore helmets of wood or metal to deflect incoming
projectiles. This armor was vital to the safety of the soldier; without it,
he was vulnerable to injury by the weapons coming against him.

Armor is external protection from physical attack. It guards the vital
organs and the head from injury. Armor is external, not internal. There
is no physical, external protection for the spirit and soul of an individual.

Armor, however, was not just defensive in nature. In addition to
what was worn, the armor included offensive weapons. The spear, sword,
and arrow were used to inflict injury on the opponent. The more skilled

the soldier in using these offensive weapons, the better his chances of survival.

Modern warfare has changed, so this type of armor is less important. However, soldiers and law enforcement officers wear protective gear such as head helmets and bulletproof vests to protect their vital organs from gunshot wounds. They wear special shoes to provide solid footing and, of course, they carry a variety of weapons.

What Is Spiritual Armor?

Spiritual armor refers to armor that operates in the spiritual realm rather than in the physical. The best-known passage of scripture relating to spiritual armor is Ephesians 6, which is where Paul speaks of the need for the armor and describes each piece. It is also mentioned in 2 Corinthians 10:3–5 (NASB):

> For though we walk in the flesh, we do not war according to the flesh, for the weapons of our warfare are not of the flesh, but divinely powerful for the destruction of fortresses. We are destroying speculations and every lofty thing raised up against the knowledge of God, and we are taking every thought captive to the obedience of Christ.

Paul makes it clear that these weapons are not of the flesh or physical but are spiritual in nature. This is because the enemy we face is not physical but spiritual. The battle really begins in the spirit and soul, not in the body. While there is a physical dimension to the battle, it is primarily spiritual in nature. It is very important to remember this when we are in a struggle. We must realize our struggle is not against a human but against spiritual forces of evil.

A further explanation and application of the spiritual armor will be covered in a later chapter.

What Is Light?

"Light is electromagnetic radiation within a certain portion of the electromagnetic spectrum. The word usually refers to visible light, which is visible to the human eye and is responsible for the sense of sight."[1]

Without light, we cannot see into the physical realm. It was light at creation that revealed the condition of the earth. Light exposes, reveals, and illuminates.

Light is often contrasted with darkness. Darkness can be described as the absence of light. But light is not the absence of darkness. Light has an "offensive" quality (e.g., light surges forth). If one enters a dark room and turns on the light, the light spreads throughout the room. It will permeate every part of the room except where it is blocked.

Light is for more than seeing. The laser is a tool that is used in many beneficial ways. It can project a light beam long distances and is used in medicine, industry, and the military. There are numerous similarities between a laser and light as spiritual armor.

What Is Spiritual Light?

Spiritual light is illumination in the spirit world. It is usually not visible in the physical world but reveals matters in the spirit world.

In the Old Testament, light is often used to describe the presence and glory of God. The word *shekinah* is used by the Hebrew Bible to describe the visible presence of God in the form of light. Numerous times in the Old Testament, God revealed his presence in the form of light. When Moses saw the burning bush, God told him that he was standing on holy ground. Throughout the journey from Egypt to Canaan, God revealed his presence as light. In the Most Holy Place in the tabernacle, God's presence was visible light.

There are similar usages in the New Testament, such as when the angels appeared to the shepherds and others. "In the New Testament, it

---

[1] Wikipedia

is the *manifestation of God's self-existent life*; divine *illumination* to reveal and impart life, through Christ."[2]

God's Word Is Light

> "Your word is a lamp for my feet, a light on my path" (Psalm 119:105).

God revealed in the scriptures is light to our lives. The Bible illuminates the soul's need for a savior and guides the believer in the paths of God.

The Power of Light

> "The light shines in the darkness, and the darkness has not overcome it" (John 1:5).

Jesus is the light that came into the world as the life of men. The devil and Jewish leaders tried to extinguish the light but were unable to do so. Even when it seemed that they were victorious with the death of Christ on the cross, the light overcame the darkness with the resurrection.

Note that the light shines in the darkness, and the darkness has not overcome it. Light overcomes darkness—darkness does not overcome light. This is true in both the natural and spiritual world. Darkness really has no power in itself. Many times, what empowers darkness is what we, as humans, give it through fear.

In a similar way, Jesus said that he would build his church, and the gates of hell would not overcome it. This truth has been evident throughout history: many have tried to outlaw the church and banish it from the world, yet time and time again they have failed.

Because God is the power source of light, there in nothing that can permanently withstand it. With this understanding, we begin to see light as a weapon for the believer to use against the enemy. It may not be visible to the physical eye, but in the spirit realm it is powerful and effective.

---

[2] *Strong's Concordance* #5457 (emphasis in original)

The armor of light is the protective presence of God over the believer. It covers and permeates the spirit, soul, and body with the brilliance of light that cannot be penetrated by an evil force.

CHAPTER 3

G⊕D IS LIGHT

God is light; in him there is no darkness at all.
—1 John 1:5

To fully understand the armor of light, it is imperative to understand the nature of God as the source of light. It is the light of God that enables the armor of light to be effective. God the Father, Jesus Christ the Son, and the Holy Spirit are all related to light in scripture.

THE NATURE ⊕F G⊕D

"God is light" (1 John 1:5).

These three words—"God is light"—are profound. Of all the ways the apostle John could have described the message from Jesus, he chose three words. They are three simple words that carry far more meaning than what is seen at first glance. "God is light" is a powerful description of his nature.

Clark's commentary gives us great insight into the meaning of God's nature:

> God is light—the source of wisdom, knowledge, holiness, and happiness; and in him is no darkness at all—no ignorance, no imperfection, no sinfulness, no

misery. And from him wisdom, knowledge, holiness, and happiness are received by every believing soul. This is the grand message of the Gospel, the great principle on which the happiness of man depends.

Light implies every essential excellence, especially wisdom, holiness, and happiness.

Darkness implies all imperfection, and principally ignorance, sinfulness, and misery.

Light is the purest, the most subtle, the most useful, and the most diffusive of all God's creatures; it is, therefore, a very proper emblem of the purity, perfection, and goodness of the Divine nature.

God is to the human soul, what the light is to the world; without the latter, all would be dismal and uncomfortable, and terror and death would universally prevail: and without an indwelling God, what is religion? Without his all-penetrating and diffusive light, what is the soul of man? Religion would be an empty science, a dead letter, a system unauthoritated and uninfluencing, and the soul a trackless wilderness, a howling waste, full of evil, of terror and dismay, and ever racked with realizing anticipations of future, successive, permanent, substantial, and endless misery. No wonder the apostle lays this down as a first and grand principle, stating it to be the essential message which he had received from Christ to deliver to the world.[3]

When one considers the qualities of light, they are descriptive of God. Light seeks to permeate everything. God took the initiative to create the world. God sought after Adam and Eve when they hid after eating the forbidden fruit. God sought out Abram, called Moses and established the law, and time and time again rescued Israel from its enemies. God designed the plan of salvation and sent Jesus as the

---

[3] *Commentary on the Bible*, by Adam Clarke [1831].Text Courtesy of Internet Sacred Texts Archive. Bible Hub

redeemer. One day he will send Jesus to return to earth and usher in a new heaven and new earth. One view of the Bible is that it is the record of a holy God seeking reconciliation with fallen humanity.

From creation to the present time, God's presence always brings revelation. It exposes the heart and reveals the motives of humanity. It exposes evil in individuals and society. Over time, the social structures and strongholds are revealed by God's light.

THE FIRST RECORDED WORDS OF GOD

> "And God said, 'Let there be light,' and there was light. God saw that the light was good, and he separated the light from the darkness. God called the light 'day,' and the darkness he called 'night.' And there was evening, and there was morning—the first day" (Genesis 1:3–5).

The first thing spoken by God was "Let there be light." The world was in darkness, and into that darkness, God spoke. Further, God separated the light from the darkness, and thus began day and night and the days of the week.

For many years, I wondered what this Genesis 1:3 light was, since the sun was not created until the fourth day. I have generally believed that all light in the natural world today comes from the sun. So what was this light?

John Morris gives the following insight: "Light is produced by friction, by fire, by numerous chemical reactions, as well as the nuclear reactions of atomic fission and fusion, which is what we think is occurring in the sun. God had at His fingertips many options to accomplish His purposes. Light does not automatically require the sun. When God created 'light' in verse 3, the word used connotes the presence of light only, while the word used for 'lights' on Day Four is best translated 'light bearers,' or permanent light sources."[4]

Is it possible that the light of the first day in creation was the very presence of God? As God was in the creative process, his presence gave

---

[4] *Sunlight Before the Sun* by John D. Morris, Ph.D.

light until the sun and stars were created as timekeepers for humanity. I think this is entirely possible, as we have seen that the very essence of God is light.

We also know that Adam and Eve were physically naked before the fall. They wore no clothes and were not ashamed. After they sinned, they realized their nakedness and tried to cover it with leaves. How did they know they were naked? Is it possible that they were clothed with light from creation as a covering, and when they sinned, that covering of light was lost and their nakedness was exposed? Is it also possible that, because of their perfection before the fall, they saw with "spiritual eyes," and when sin came, they lost that spiritual vision, and physical nakedness was revealed?

God Is Light

The scripture gives many examples of how God is light and the implications of that light. Consider the following:

- **The Glory of God's Dwelling Place.** "God [is] the blessed and only Ruler, the King of kings and Lord of lords, who alone is immortal and who lives in *unapproachable light*, whom no-one has seen or can see. To him be honor and might forever. Amen" (1 Timothy 6:15–16).
- **The Nature of God.** "Every good and perfect gift is from above, coming down from the Father of the heavenly lights, who does not change like shifting shadows" (James 1:17).
- **God's Favor.** "Many, LORD, are asking, "Who will bring us prosperity?" Let the light of your face shine on us." (Psalm 4:6)
- **God's Guidance.** "How I long for the months gone by, for the days when God watched over me, when his lamp shone upon my head and by his *light* I walked through darkness!" (Job 29:2–3).
- **God's Presence.** "Blessed are those who have learned to acclaim you, who walk in *the light of your presence*, LORD" (Psalm 89:15).
- **God's Presence and Protection.** God's presence and protection was with the Israelites during their journey in the desert. The cloud by day and pillar of fire at night was the very presence

of God (Exodus 14:19–20). This will be explored in the next chapter.

- **God Is Clothed with Light.** "The LORD wraps himself in *light* as with a garment; he stretches out the heavens like a tent" (Psalm 104:2); "You are radiant with *light*, more majestic than mountains rich with game" (Psalm 76:4).

- **God's Illumination.** The tabernacle constructed by Moses in the desert housed the Most Holy Place, which was a fifteen-foot square room which subsequently housed the Ark of the Covenant covered by the mercy seat. Once a year, the high priest entered this room to offer the blood sacrifice. This room had no windows. The entrance was covered with animal skins. When the Hebrews erected the tabernacle and everything was in order, the presence of God would come down and fill that room. Consequently, it was filled with light. This was the *shekinah* glory. Other verses that relate to God's illumination: "In your *light* we see light" (Psalm 36:9); "For it is *light* that makes everything visible. This is why it is said: 'Wake up, O sleeper, rise from the dead, and Christ will shine on you'" (Ephesians 5:14 [version]).

Regarding the *shekinah* glory:

> In the Old Testament times, this presence of God is referred to as the Shekinah glory. While Shekinah is not a biblical word, it describes the glory of God in the form of light. Throughout the Bible, YEHOVAH God speaks of His desire for an intimate relationship with His people. The "shekinah," therefore, refers to the presence of YEHOVAH that was—but is not now—physically manifested in the time-space continuum. It could be seen. The presence was A VEHICLE OF THE PERSON OF YEHOVAH GOD IN THE THREE DIMENSIONAL WORLD. Solomon's understanding that YEHOVAH cannot actually be limited to Temples on earth because of His eternal nature can be seen in

> I Kings 8:27—"But will God really dwell [yashav] on earth? Even the heavens to their utmost reaches cannot contain You, how much less this House [Temple] that I have built!"[5]

These verses, and more, reveal the character of God as light. The light of his presence provides guidance and protection to the believer.

JESUS IS THE LIGHT

As a part of the Godhead, Jesus is described as light: "In the beginning was the Word, and the Word was with God, and the Word was God. He was with God in the beginning. Through him all things were made; without him nothing was made that has been made. In him was life, and that life was the *light* of all mankind. The light shines in the darkness, and the darkness has not overcome it" (John 1:1–5).

The *People's New Testament* gives the following excellent explanation of Christ as light: "The life was the light of men. The life that Christ bestows enlightens men. He is the Light of the World (John 8:12; 9:5). His light chases away the darkness of the earth, though, when John wrote, the darkness did not receive it. Men, in darkness, had eyes and saw not. All history demonstrates that Christ is the Light of the World; every redeemed soul recognizes that."

Jesus himself declared that he is the light of the world: "I am the light of the world. Whoever follows me will never walk in darkness, but will have the light of life" (John 8:12); "I will not say much more to you, for the prince of this world is coming. He has no hold over me" (John 14:30).

How was it that the evil one had no hold over Jesus? As the light of the world, who lived a sinless life, it was impossible for the evil one to have any grip on Christ. His light was so powerful that the enemy could get no foothold.

Jesus Christ was present at creation when God said, "Let there be light." We will see in the next chapter that he was present on the journey from Egypt to Canaan. His ministry on earth was one of revealing the

---

5 http://hope-of-israel.org.nz

true nature of the Father to a people who misunderstood his love and compassion. He exposed the hearts of the religious leaders and through his death defeated the darkness of evil.

THE HOLY SPIRIT AS LIGHT

While there are no specific references to the Holy Spirit as light in the same way as for God the Father and Jesus the Son, nevertheless, the Spirit functions as light to the believer.

In John 14:26, Jesus tells the disciples that "the Advocate, the Holy Spirit, whom the Father will send in my name, will teach you all things and will remind you of everything I have said to you."

The Spirit would teach and remind the disciples of what Jesus taught them. This is another way of saying he will reveal things to us, which is one function of light.

Paul put it this way in Ephesians 1:17: "I keep asking that the God of our Lord Jesus Christ, the glorious Father, may give you the Spirit of wisdom and revelation, so that you may know him better." Paul specifically names him as the Spirit of revelation!

Further, on the day of Pentecost, as the believers were gathered in the upper room, the Holy Spirit came upon them in the form of tongues of fire, a manifestation of light.

Thus, the very nature of God revealed as Father, Son, and Holy Spirit, is manifest as light in each Person's relation to humans.

God's presence as light had an effect on those in his presence. When Moses came down the mountain from being in the presence of God for forty days, his face shone with such a bright light that he had to cover his face so the people could look at him. The disciples, on the Mount of Transfiguration, saw Jesus in brilliant light as he spoke with Moses and Elijah.

When Saul was traveling to Damascus to arrest Christians, he and his companions were struck down by a bright light, and then the Lord Jesus spoke to him. When Jesus appeared in a vision to John, as recorded in Revelation, his face was like the sun shining in all its brilliance. Later in Revelation we read that in the new city there is no need for the sun, for the glory of God gives it light, and the Lamb (Jesus) is its lamp.

The Holy Spirit appeared to the post-resurrection believers as tongues of fire and the revealer of truth. The Holy Spirit empowered the disciples as witnesses, and the church age began.

There are more than thirty direct references in scripture to God and Christ being light. The Father, Son, and Holy Spirit, as the Godhead, are spoken of as being in their very nature light and as being a source of light.

Since light is such a powerful manifestation of God, it is no wonder that Satan seeks to transform himself into an angel of light (2 Corinthians 11:14). He knows the awesome and powerful aspect of God's light and seeks to deceive God's followers as counterfeit light. Remember, something can only be a counterfeit in imitation of the genuine article. Satan would not seek to present himself as light if God were not the true light. This is a powerful testimony to God's very nature being light.

The wonderful truth about our God being this powerful being and source of light is that he is all things for us. This is not for himself to revel in, but he is all this for his children. In fact, the scriptures refer to believers as "children of light."

In speaking of the "day of the Lord" at the end of the present age, Paul reminds us that we are children of the light and of the day; therefore we will not be deceived as others:

> But you, brothers and sisters, are not in darkness so that this day should surprise you like a thief. You are all children of the light and children of the day. We do not belong to the night or to the darkness. So then, let us not be like others, who are asleep, but let us be awake and sober. For those who sleep, sleep at night, and those who get drunk, get drunk at night. But since we belong to the day, let us be sober, putting on faith and love as a breastplate, and the hope of salvation as a helmet. For God did not appoint us to suffer wrath but to receive salvation through our Lord Jesus Christ. (1 Thessalonians 5:4–9)

The very nature of God is light. Hallelujah—what a great God we serve!

CHAPTER 4

PROTECTION AND DIRECTION

By day the LORD went ahead of them in a pillar of cloud to
guide them on their way and by night in a pillar of fire to
give them light, so that they could travel by day or night.
—*Exodus 13:21*

With an understanding that God is light and that light is central
to salvation and our Christian life, we now turn our attention
to a biblical example of how God's presence as light provided direction
and protection for his people.

When God delivered his people from bondage in Egypt, he led
them through the desert toward the Promised Land. This was a difficult
and dangerous journey. There was extreme heat during the day, cold at
night, and scarcity of food and water. They needed to know the way to
go and have protection from the elements. Perhaps Moses knew the path
through the desert, having lived there for forty years, but no one else
would have had experience traveling in those lands.

DIRECTION

God provided direction and protection in a unique and profound way.
In Exodus 13, we read that there was a cloud to lead them in the day
and fire to lead them at night. They followed as the cloud moved during
the day. Some also think that when they first left Egypt, they may have

traveled day and night to put as much distance as possible between them and Egypt. Nighttime travel would have been possible with the fire leading the way.

It was not unusual to have a cloud and fire accompany a march. It was common for fire to lead armies:

> The Persians and Greeks used fire and smoke as signals in their marches, and in a well-known papyrus, the commander of an Egyptian expedition is called "A flame in the darkness at the head of his soldiers." By this sign then of the pillar of cloud, the Lord showed Himself as their leader and general.[6]
>
> The Persians would carry vessels with fire in them which they called sacred and eternal, in silver altars, in front of the army.[7]

As with the plagues, God used something that the Egyptians were familiar with and turned it for his own purpose. With the cloud and fire, he showed the Israelites the way through the desert toward their final destination. Of course, it had the downside of allowing Pharaoh and his army to see where they were going when the king decided to bring them back to Egypt. But God took care of that at the Red Sea.

PROTECTION

In addition to direction, this cloud and fire provided protection. The desert sun was scorching hot during the day, and nighttime temperatures would plummet. The cloud and fire provided a protective shield from the sun in the daytime and warmth at night. Adam Clarke adds an additional insight that is interesting regarding the cloud and fire: the cloud caused humid conditions that provided moisture for them.

---

[6] *Barnes Notes, Notes on the Bible* by Albert Barnes [1834].Text Courtesy of Internet Sacred Texts Archive.

[7] *Biblical Commentary on the Old Testament*, by Carl Friedrich Keil and Franz Delitzsch [1857–78]. Text Courtesy of Internet Sacred Texts Archive. Bible Hub

> It was a covering for them during the day, and preserved them from the scorching rays of the sun; and supplied them with a sufficiency of aqueous particles, not only to cool that burning atmosphere, but to give refreshment to themselves and their cattle; and its humidity was so abundant that the apostle here represents the people as thoroughly sprinkled and enveloped in its aqueous vapour.[8]

Our God is indeed a God of detail and compassion. He, being the creator, knew the conditions they would face, so he sent a cloud and fire. They provided direction, light, and protection from both heat and sun by day, and gave warmth at night.

What Was This Cloud and Fire?

This provision was more than physical in nature. A natural cloud and fire would have served their purposes well, but this was divine provision. Exodus 13:21 states that "the LORD went ahead of them." This cloud and fire was the very presence of the Lord in the form of cloud and fire. Again I quote Clarke's commentary: "This pillar or column, which appeared as a cloud by day, and a fire by night, was the symbol of the Divine presence. This was the Shechinah [sic] or Divine dwelling place, and was the continual proof of the presence and protection of God."

This glory of God as a cloud or light was present with them throughout their wilderness journey. It led and protected them. When they built the tabernacle, it filled the Holy of Holies. When the cloud lifted from the tabernacle, they packed it up, and when the cloud moved, they followed.

A Closer Look

Let's take a closer look at the protection God provided them. When the Israelites were at the Red Sea and Pharaoh's army was approaching,

---

[8] *Commentary on the Bible*, by Adam Clarke [1831].Text Courtesy of Internet Sacred Texts Archive. Bible Hub

they were literally caught between the sea ahead of them and the army behind. Humanly speaking, there was no way to escape. But again, a caring God made a way.

> Then *the angel of God*, who had been traveling in front of Israel's army, withdrew and went behind them. The pillar of cloud also moved from in front and stood behind them. (Exodus 14:19)

Who Is This Angel of God?

When God called Moses through the burning bush, note what scripture says:

> There the angel of the LORD appeared to him in flames of fire from within a bush. Moses saw that though the bush was on fire it did not burn up. So Moses thought, "I will go over and see this strange sight— why the bush does not burn up."
>
> When the LORD saw that he had gone over to look, God called to him from within the bush, "Moses! Moses!"
>
> And Moses said, "Here I am."
>
> "Do not come any closer," God said. "Take off your sandals, for the place where you are standing is holy ground." Then he said, "I am the God of your father, the God of Abraham, the God of Isaac and the God of Jacob." At this, Moses hid his face, because he was afraid to look at God. (Exodus 3:2-6

The angel of the Lord appeared to Moses in the flames and identified himself as the God of his fathers.

> It is clear from this abundance of evidence that the angel of the Lord in the Old Testament was a pre-incarnate form of our Lord Jesus Christ, who would

later permanently take on flesh when he came as a babe in Bethlehem.[9]

This manifestation by the Lord is known as a *theophany*, the appearance of the Lord Jesus as an angel. The phrase in the Old Testament is "the angel of the Lord." It was the presence of the Lord Jesus himself.

Another passage from Exodus also gives clarity to the difference between "an angel" and "the angel of the Lord" as the presence of Christ. In Exodus 33, God tells Moses to leave this place and go the Promised Land:

> I will send *an angel* before you and drive out the Canaanites, Amorites, Hittites, Perizzites, Hivites and Jebusites. Go up to the land flowing with milk and honey. But *I will not go with you*, because you are a stiff-necked people and I might destroy you on the way. (Exodus 33:2–3)

Later in the conversation Moses appeals to God to know who will go with him:

> Moses said to the LORD, "You have been telling me, 'Lead these people,' but you have not let me know whom you will send with me. You have said, 'I know you by name and you have found favor with me.'" (Exodus 33:12)

> The LORD replied, "My Presence will go with you, and I will give you rest."

> Then Moses said to him, "If your Presence does not go with us, do not send us up from here." (Exodus 33:14–15)

---

[9] *Hard Sayings of the Bible* by Walter C. Kaiser Jr., Peter H. Davids, F. F. Bruce, and Manfred T. Brauch, InterVarsity Press, Downers Grove, IL

Exodus 14:19 states that *the angel of God* was traveling in front of the Israel's army. In chapter 33, God says that *an angel* will go with Moses but that he would not go with them. Later, God relents and says that his presence will go with them.

I conclude from this that "the angel of the Lord" who was traveling with the people on the journey to the Red Sea was indeed the very presence of God, while "an angel," whom God was intending to send with them as they left Sinai, was not the Lord himself but one of his angels.

DIVINE PROTECTION

Back to the dilemma at the Red Sea. The sea was in front of the people, and the army was coming from behind. As they faced this impossible situation, God did something remarkable.

> Then the angel of God, who had been traveling in front of Israel's army, withdrew and went behind them. The pillar of cloud also moved from in front and stood behind them, coming between the armies of Egypt and Israel. Throughout the night the cloud brought darkness to the one side and light to the other side; so neither went near the other all night long. (Exodus 14:19–20)

The angel moved from in front of them to the back. The pillar moved from in front to the back, and the cloud moved from in front to the back. Through the night, the cloud provided darkness to one side and light to the other

That is protection! The Egyptian army could not see the Israelites, and the Israelites had both light and the warmth of the fire.

> Then Moses stretched out his hand over the sea, and all that night the LORD drove the sea back with a strong east wind and turned it into dry land. The waters were divided, and the Israelites went through the sea on dry

ground, with a wall of water on their right and on their left. (Exodus 14:21–22)

God drove back the water so the people could cross the sea on dry land.

> The Egyptians pursued them, and all Pharaoh's horses and chariots and horsemen followed them into the sea. During the last watch of the night, *the Lord looked down* from the pillar of fire and cloud at the Egyptian army and threw it into confusion. He jammed the wheels of their chariots so that they had difficulty driving. And the Egyptians said, "Let's get away from the Israelites! The Lord is fighting for them against Egypt." (Exodus 14:23–25)

The Egyptian army pursued the people into the sea. But note that the Lord looked down from the fire and cloud. Again, who was in this fire and cloud? The Lord Almighty. This fire and cloud were the presence of the Lord with a physical manifestation. The Lord was present with his people. He saw them just as he saw Moses when the bush was on fire. We have a personal God who sees us in our need.

He not only saw them, he did something about their need. He jammed the wheels of the chariots so that they could not continue the pursuit. What a great God!

His presence was both direction and protection. Without his intervention, the Hebrews would have undoubtedly been captured by the Egyptian army and forced to return to captivity. This is a powerful example of who the Lord has been to his people throughout history and continues to be today.

Armor of Light

When we put on the armor of light, this is what we put on! The presence of the Lord as light is our armor of defense. We have this same protection today as Israel did. The God who was in the cloud and fire is with us today! He is the same yesterday, today, and forever.

When we put on the armor of light, we have direction and protection. In the next chapter, we will examine this more closely.

CHAPTER 5

PUT ON THE ARMOR

Put on the armor of light.
—*Romans 13:12*

The armor of light is the presence of the Lord with us. When we put on the armor of light, we are clothed with the presence of almighty God. He is our armor of defense. We have the same protection for us today as Israel did in the desert. The God who was in the cloud and the fire is with us today! He is the same yesterday, today, and forever. As we have seen, it is the Father, Son, and Holy Spirit who is our armor against the evil one.

DIRECTION

When we put on the armor of light, we have direction for our lives. We have light to guide our way through life. The light of the Lord shines on our pathway. As the light led Moses, so the light of the Lord directs us as well. His light is received though the Word of God, which is a light to our way and lamp for our feet. It is the voice of the Holy Spirit saying "This is the way; walk in it" (Isaiah 30:21).

> But if we walk in the light, as he is in the light, we have fellowship with one another, and the blood of Jesus, his Son, purifies us from all sin. (1 John 1:7)

Walking in light is to walk in obedience to God's will and Word. The result is fellowship and cleansing. As we have fellowship with God and with others, we receive godly counsel and direction for life. We do not stumble in the darkness of sin and unbelief but go through life with confidence in the Lord's leading

There are times when I picture a spotlight like those used to highlight an actor on stage, shining ahead of me. As I walk in that light, I am in the will of God. When the light moves, I move; when the light stops, I stop—just as the Israelites did, following the cloud in the desert.

PROTECTION

The light is protection from the evil one. Just as the cloud shielded the Hebrews so the Egyptians could not see them, the armor of light is a shield around us for protection. With the armor, there is a separation between us and Satan. I am not saying that he cannot see us, but I believe that he cannot touch us without the permission of God, and God limits him.

Job was only afflicted to the degree that God allowed. There was a limit to what Satan could do to him. We have that same kind of protection today. Job was not aware of it, but we are. We have much more insight and understanding than he did because we have the completed scriptures and the Holy Spirit living within us.

This covering is not necessarily over our physical bodies but is over our soul and spirit. The armor of light is for the spiritual battle in which we are engaged. It covers the most important part of us: the soul and the spirit. God, in his mercy, may extend the protection to our physical bodies, but I find no guarantee of that in scripture. That does not mean we should not pray for and expect physical protection, but we need to realize that we live in a fallen world, and our bodies are subject to the realities of the physical world.

The presence of God is with us. He watches over us as he did over the Israelites going through the sea. He sees our lives, he feels our pain, he knows our enemy, and he sees what is before us and what is coming behind us. As a pillar of fire, a wall of protection, and a canopy over us, he is our protector.

There are numerous biblical examples as a precedent for this understanding. Zechariah described a vision of the city of Jerusalem with a wall of fire:

> Then the angel who was speaking to me left, and another angel came to meet him and said to him: "Run, tell that young man, 'Jerusalem will be a city without walls because of the great number of men and livestock in it. And I myself will be *a wall of fire* around it,' declares the Lord, 'and I will be *its glory within*.'" (Zechariah 2:3–5 NIV 1984)

The Lord will be a wall of fire! His glory will be within the city. Later, he says whoever touches us touches the apple of his eye.

> Then the Lord will create over all of Mount Zion and over those who assemble there a cloud of smoke by day and a glow of *flaming fire* by night; over everything the *glory will be a canopy.* It will be a shelter and shade from the heat of the day, and a refuge and hiding-place from the storm and rain. (Isaiah 4:5–6)

> "No weapon that is formed against you will prosper; and every tongue that accuses you in judgment you will condemn. This is the heritage of the servants of the Lord, and their vindication is from Me," declares the Lord. (Isaiah 54:17 NASB)

Consider Elisha's protection in 2 Kings 6:14–17. The Arameans were attacking Israel and sent an army to capture Elisha because he had given the king of Israel information about the location of their army.

> When the servant of the man of God got up and went out early the next morning, an army with horses and chariots had surrounded the city. "Oh no, my lord! What shall we do?' the servant asked.

"Don't be afraid," the prophet answered. "Those who are
with us are more than those who are with them." And
Elisha prayed, "Open his eyes, LORD, so that he may
see." Then the LORD opened the servant's eyes, and he
looked and saw the hills full of horses and *chariots of fire*
all around Elisha. (2 Kings 6:15–17)

When the Lord opened the servant's eyes, he saw horses and chariots
of fire. This was God's protection over Elisha! This protection was not
visible to the human eye until God allowed the servant to see it. There
are angels around us whom we do not see with our human eye. While
these were probably holy angels appearing as horses and chariots, they
symbolize God's protection (cf. Psalm 91).

David understood this protection and wrote many psalms about it.

The LORD is my *light* and my salvation—
    whom shall I fear?
The LORD is the stronghold of my life—
    of whom shall I be afraid?
When evil men advance against me
    to devour my flesh,
when my enemies and my foes attack me,
    they will stumble and fall.
Though an army besiege me,
    my heart will not fear;
though war break out against me,
    even then will I be confident. (Psalm 27:1–3)

Praise the LORD, O my soul.
O LORD my God, you are very great;
    you are clothed with splendor and majesty.
He wraps himself in *light* as with a garment;
    he stretches out the heavens like a tent. (Psalm 104:1–2)

The Lord is our light and our protection. The Lord God Almighty
is our true defense and protection from evil. As I mentioned in the first

chapter, in the past fifty-plus years, our culture has undergone significant changes as a result of occult activity directly targeted on releasing darkness upon us. Western culture has become a culture that calls good evil and evil good. We have spiritual armor to stand against this evil. We have the power to withstand this attack and be victorious. There is no need for the believer to become overwhelmed by evil or to fear!

We live in evil times that require vigilance on our part. Through today's music, Internet, TV, friends, books, movies, role-playing video games, and attacks from the enemy, we are exposed to detrimental spiritual influences every day. Our sin makes us vulnerable. When we give ourselves over to sinful habits, we come under spiritual influences. These can become strongholds and bring us under the control of the world, the flesh, and the adversary. The flesh will always side with the adversary because the flesh is selfish and wants what it wants! There is no peace for a believer in this condition.

Jesus describes our enemy in John 10:10 as the "thief [who] comes only to steal and kill and destroy." The enemy's objective is to steal your peace, kill your joy, and destroy your testimony.

Peter described him this way: "Be self-controlled and alert. Your enemy the devil prowls around like a roaring lion looking for someone to devour. Resist him, standing firm in the faith, because you know that your brothers throughout the world are undergoing the same kind of sufferings" (1 Peter 5:8–9 NIV 1984). We cannot be passive, or we will be overwhelmed. The enemy is on the prowl, so we need to resist him. No fear. No doubt. Doubt drives holes through our armor!

We are at war, every day, against the world, the flesh, and the adversary. When we became followers of Jesus, we signed up for his army, and God gave us armor. The Christian who does not dress in the armor of light is naked and exposed to enemy attack. Such a Christian is fighting in the flesh, in his or her own strength. Predatory occultists target defenseless Christians who are too weak to withstand their advances. These predators (and we will never know who they are) make examples of naked believers to prove that our God is nothing. It is vital that we cover ourselves daily with this armor and stand firm.

Curses and generational strongholds can also affect believers. A curse invokes supernatural power to harm someone or something. A generational curse or stronghold is a deeply held pattern of beliefs and behaviors that are passed down from one generation to the next. The armor of light is a defense against them.

> In all these things we are more than conquerors through him who loved us. (Romans 8:37)

As believers in the Lord Jesus, we have the Holy Spirit within us. We have the power of God with us at all times! When Jesus said he would never leave us, he was referring to the Holy Spirit who is always with the believer. We are more than conquerors! We not only can be victorious, but because of the power of God, we *are* victorious over the enemy. We have to *believe* it! Even if we can't *see* it or *feel* it, we have to believe it!

> You are all children of the light and children of the day. We do not belong to the night or to the darkness. (1 Thessalonians 5:5)

We are children of the day, meaning we walk in light. We are not walking according to the darkness of ignorance and disobedience. We walk in the light of the scriptures and the revelation by the Spirit. The armor of light is both direction in life and protection from the darkness of the world. We don't belong to the darkness or owe allegiance to dark forces. We do not listen to the lies of the devil so that we are deceived.

Because the armor is spiritual in nature, it can be seen by enemy spiritual forces. Just as the fire and cloud prevented Pharaoh from seeing the Israelites, the armor of light can either prevent the enemy from seeing us or present such a bright light that they cannot stand in its presence.

Again, remember that this is spiritual and not physical light. This may also be why we don't see the need to put on armor: the spiritual is not visible to the physical eye. However, if our eyes were adjusted just a little, we would see into the spirit world and see things that would astound us. This is the realm where both the angels of God and the demons operate. When we put on the armor, we are helping to empower the angels in their battle against evil forces.

Must We Put It On?

All these truths recall an earlier question: if all the above is true, then why do we have to put on the armor of light? Is it not automatically ours when we confess Christ? Since the armor is in reality the presence of God, and he will never leave us, then what happens that we need to keep putting on the armor?

All the armor is indeed ours. However, as with other spiritual principles, we must confess it with our mouth to activate it. Consider the familiar passage from Romans 10:9–10: "If you declare with your mouth, 'Jesus is Lord,' and believe in your heart that God raised him from the dead, you will be saved. For it is with your heart that you believe and are justified, and it is with your mouth that you profess your faith and are saved." Our salvation is effective only when we believe *and* profess. It is the confession with our mouth that activates the belief. The same is true for putting on armor. We can believe it, but it is activated by confession.

Confession does several other things as well. When we confess with our mouth, we hear ourselves say it. This is an audible message to us that we have direction and protection. When you hear yourself say something, it serves as a reminder.

Voicing aloud our belief also can be heard by the enemy, and it is a reminder to him that he has no power in us. Remember that the evil one only has as much power over us as we give him. He was defeated by Christ on the cross. It is our fear and unbelief that empower him. When we confess with our mouth the presence and glory of God, we weaken him and render him powerless.

Also, at night, it is true in a sense that when we are asleep, we are not in executive control of our minds. It may be that the enemy then sows seeds of fear, doubt, unbelief, and other things into our minds that take root and are acted upon the next day. Therefore, this is a good reason to pray protection over our minds when we sleep and again in the morning upon rising.

Some think that we are automatically protected as Christians by the blood of Jesus. It is true that the blood of Jesus covers us as believers, but that covering is a covering of our sin. The blood of Christ is the means whereby we are forgiven. A careful examination of scriptures will show that the verses that speak of Christ's blood all refer to forgiveness and cleansing. I used to think there was a hedge of blood protection around us. However I cannot find scripture that substantiates that. Revelation 12:11 mentions those who overcame Satan by the blood of the Lamb. Their victory was not in their own righteousness or power but that of the blood of the sinless Son of God, who defeated Satan on the cross through the shedding of his blood. Barnes notes it this way, "The blood of Christ was that by which they were redeemed, and it was in virtue of the efficacy of the atonement that they were enabled to achieve the victory."

This in no way diminishes the importance of the blood of Jesus. The fact is that unless Christians are covered by the blood, they cannot be covered with the armor of light. The blood covers sin; the light covers darkness.

PUT ⊕N THE ARⅿ⊕R

We put on the armor of light through prayer and confession. We put on the armor of light by verbally covering ourselves with light. We can be intentional about protection by praying prayers of protection. Because of the influences we face, we need to do this daily. You can pray for yourself, your spouse, your children, grandchildren, and others. Here is a sample prayer:

God, I come to you in the name of Jesus to confess that he is my Savior and Lord. I thank you that you have brought me from the darkness into the light. My spirit surrenders to the Holy Spirit as I put on the armor of light by wrapping myself in the light of your presence. I cover my spirit, soul, and body with the glorious light of your presence. I thank you that your glory is a shield around me and that I am protected from all the power of the enemy.

Prayer 'For' – Not Prayer 'Against'

This way of praying is proactive and not reactive. It is praying positively, not negatively. It is praying *for* God's protection and not *against* the devil.

A church I pastored went to the Bowery Mission in New York City each year. We would leave in the afternoon and arrive at the mission well before the service. Staff there would give tours of the building, explaining the program. The director would then invite us to pray for the upcoming service.

One year as we, as a church, were beginning to understand our position in Christ and our authority over the devil, we prayed strong prayers against the devil. We boldly told him that he had no power over the service and the men who would gather. This went on for some time and we thought we had a really good prayer meeting and went into the service expecting great things to happen.

The service did not go as expected. The music and preaching were okay, but something didn't seem quite right. The bigger disappointment was the lack of response to the altar call. Usually, many men would respond to the invitation to confess Christ and begin the Christian life. That evening, I think one man came forward. We were very disappointed.

Later, on the way home as we were riding the Staten Island Ferry, I looked back over the city. I said, "Lord, what happened this evening? We prepared for the service, we prayed powerful prayers, so why the lack of response?"

The response of God was this: "You spent more time talking to the devil before the service than you did talking to me." Wow, what a revelation. As I reflected on our prayer time, it was true. The focus on taking authority over the devil consumed more prayers than positive praying for the Lord to work.

That was a lesson I never forgot. While I do believe that we have authority over Satan, and there are times to exercise that, I believe sometimes we spend too much time praying against the devil and not enough time interceding for the Lord to display his divine power.

I have found that praying the armor of light is one way to be positive and proactive in prayer. It takes the focus off the enemy and places it on the Lord, who is really the source of our help. This is especially understood by those who have experienced spiritual abuse and have greater sensitivity to the spirit world. These persons testify to the protection they sense when putting on the armor of light.

As with all spiritual dynamics, not all persons experience spiritual reality in the same way. Some can see into the spirit realm; some feel the spiritual realm. Others walk through life by faith; believing the reality they may not see or feel, they have a knowing in their spirit. These are varying expressions of our Christian walk. One is not right or better than another, but simply the way the Lord has chosen for us to experience the reality of his presence.

The same is true for the armor of light. Not all persons will experience it the same way. For some it may be somewhat tangible; for others it is purely a walk of trust. What is important is not how we experience it but whether we obediently put it on and trust the Lord to provide the direction and protection.

CHAPTER 6

PUT ON THE FULL ARMOR

Put on the full armor of God,
so that you can take your stand against the devil's schemes.
—*Ephesians 6:11*

The armor of light is directly related to the spiritual armor listed by Paul in Ephesians 6. The Ephesians passage lists in detail the actual weapons of our warfare against evil. Many books have been written about this armor, so it in not our intent here to go into detail. Rather we will show how the various pieces of armor relate to the armor of light.

Again, it is wise to recall that we are in a spiritual battle, not a physical one. Therefore, the weapons are spiritual and not carnal. "Though we live in the world, we do not wage war as the world does. The weapons we fight with are not the weapons of the world. On the contrary, they have divine power to demolish strongholds" (2 Corinthians 10:3–4).

Paul uses the imagery of a Roman soldier equipped for battle. He details the various pieces of armor as a way of clarifying how we fight the enemy. As we briefly examine each piece of this armor, we will see how each one represents an aspect of Christ's ministry.

BELT OF TRUTH

The belt was fastened around the waist, and it held up and kept the other pieces of armor in place. Specifically, it held the sword.

Spiritually, the belt of truth does the same thing. Without the truth, we are subject to the lies of the enemy and are open to deception. Pilate asked Jesus "What is truth?" We ask the same question, and Jesus answers in John 14:6: "I am the way and the *truth* and the life. No one comes to the Father except through me."

Truth is a proper belief of what is true or that which is correct by a standard. That standard is the Word of God. Jesus declared in John 17:17 that the Word of God is truth. The Word and the truth come together in Jesus Christ.

When we put on the belt of truth, we put on the Lord Jesus.

BREASTPLATE ⊕F RIGHTE⊕USNESS

The breastplate was a central part of the Roman soldier's armor. The breastplate protects the vital organs in the chest. It covers the ribs from injury and prevents puncture of the heart, lungs, and other inward parts.

Spiritually, it is a covering of righteousness. This righteousness is not our own but the righteousness of God, given us through Jesus Christ. Our righteousness is totally ineffective to protect from attack. Our righteousness is as dirty rags in the sight of God and is of no spiritual value. Therefore, God made Christ be sin for us that we might become righteous. This perfect righteousness of Christ is the effective armor against spiritual attack.

> It is because of him that you are in Christ Jesus, who has become for us wisdom from God – that is, our *righteousness*, holiness and redemption. (1 Corinthians 1:30)

Without righteousness, we leave ourselves open to almost certain death. When righteousness is our breastplate, the attacks of our enemy are thwarted. Righteousness has to do with our character and right living. For the Roman soldier, the breastplate was the protection of his vital organs. For us, it also our protection as we put on Christ's righteousness.

When we put on the breastplate of righteousness, we put on the Lord Jesus.

Shoes of the Gospel of Peace

Shoes provide a sure foundation for our body. Without proper shoes, we slip; our feet can be cut by stones and attacked by snakes or insets.

The gospel of peace is the good news that, as humans, we can live at peace with God and with others. Because of sin we are the enemies of God. Through Jesus Christ, we are at peace with God. Because of selfishness, certain people in our lives may be our enemies. Through Christ, we can live at peace with everyone.

The shoes of the Roman soldier enabled him to stand firm in battle. The shoes of peace enable us to stand firm in the battle with the enemy. We stand because we know we are at peace with God and with others.

For he himself is our *peace* …. (Ephesians 2:14)

When we put on the shoes of peace, we put on the Lord Jesus.

Shield of Faith

The Roman shield was a very large, slightly curved rectangular shield featuring at its center a large metal knob. With the shield, they could deflect incoming arrows.

Faith is the evidence of what we do not see (Hebrews 11:1). It is confidence in what is invisible. It is the belief that there is a God and that all he says is true. It is taking God at his word and acting accordingly. The shield of faith is our confidence in God and in the finished work of Christ. As we battle the enemy when he throws the flaming arrows of doubt, fear, lies, and unbelief, we deflect them with the confidence we have in God and his word. Notice the shield *puts out* the flaming arrows. The shield does not just repel them but extinguishes them.

Another interesting insight about the shield is that Roman soldiers would stand in a square. Those on the outside would lock arms with their shields up, making a wall. Those on the inside would hold their shields overhead for protection. The result was a formidable human tank that could be stopped only by a tremendous effort.

There is a great lesson there for us. We cannot battle the enemy alone! As believers, we need to stand together to defend ourselves from enemy attacks.

The Roman soldier used his shield to deflect the arrows of the enemy. As Christians, we use the shield of faith to deflect the enemy arrows. It is our faith that gives us the victory.

> [Let us fix] our eyes on Jesus, the pioneer and perfecter
> of *faith*. (Hebrews 12:2)

Christ is the object of our faith. According to Romans 12:3, we each have been given a measure of faith.

When we take up the shield of faith, we are taking up Jesus Christ

HELMET OF SALVATION

The helmet is protection for the head. The head is the most exposed and vulnerable part of our body. It is also the most important because it contains the brain, which controls the rest of the body.

The spiritual helmet is our salvation. It is the confidence that we are in Christ and that Christ is in us. It is the certainty that our sin is forgiven and we are in a right relationship with God through Jesus Christ.

Jesus is our salvation. There is no other way to the Father except through Jesus. By his death, resurrection, and ascension, Christ secured eternal salvation for anyone and everyone who will believe on him.

> *Salvation* is found in no one else, for there is no other
> name under heaven given to mankind by which we must
> be saved. (Acts 4:12)

The helmet of the Roman soldier protected his head from enemy blows. The helmet of salvation is our protection of our mind. Jesus is our salvation

When we put on the helmet of salvation, we put on Jesus Christ

SWORD OF THE SPIRIT

The sword of the Roman soldier was his weapon to inflict injury on his opponent. It was used in hand-to-hand combat.

The sword of the believer is our only offensive weapon. The others mentioned are for protection and defense. The sword of the Spirit is the Word of God. God's Word is truth, plain and simple. We can have perfect confidence in the fact that His words are accurate, true, and unerring. When followed, they guide us without fail in the paths that we need to walk.

> For the *word of God* is living and powerful, and sharper than any two-edged sword, piercing even to the division of soul and spirit, and of joints and marrow, and is a discerner of the thoughts and intents of the heart. (Hebrews 4:12 NKJV)

Jesus used the Word of God to overcome the temptation of the devil in the wilderness when he said, "It is written," and quoted the scriptures. This is how we use this weapon as well. When we quote the scriptures to the devil, he must leave us.

The Roman soldier used the sword in close fighting. We use the sword of God's Word to defeat the devil's attacks.

When we take up the sword of the spirit, we take up Jesus Christ.

So it becomes clear that the weapons of our warfare are—in reality—the Lord Jesus Christ. Through his earthly ministry, he overcame the evil one, and now, through him, we too have victory.

There is another important aspect of these weapons. There have been times when I prayed, "Lord, I put on the helmet of salvation, I put on the breastplate of righteousness," and so on. I meant well when doing that, and to some extent, it is effective. However, putting on the armor is more than words. It is actually using the weapon at the moment of attack. (Several versions translate Ephesians 6:13 as saying, "Take up the armor of God"—put it to use.)

It is one thing to believe that quoting the scripture will defeat the devil, but it is quite another to actually do it. It's one thing to believe that the shield of faith will protect us, but when in battle, we need to stand firm and trust in the Lord for our deliverance. The same is true with all these weapons. It's about more than belief or lip service; it is about putting them into action at the moment of need.

These weapons, then, are the weapons of light. Since the armor of light is the presence of Jesus Christ, then by putting on the Lord Jesus when in battle, we are putting on the armor of light.

When we put on this armor, we are putting on the Lord Jesus, for he is all these things to and for us. Furthermore, as we have seen previously, he is the light, so when we put on this armor, we are putting on the Lord Jesus, who is light.

PRAYER FOR PUTTING ON THE WHOLE ARMOR

God Almighty, I thank you for the provision you have made for my freedom and victory. Lord, I put on the armor of light. I cover myself with the light of your presence and glory. I put on the armor of light as the helmet of salvation, for Jesus is my salvation. I put on the armor of light as the breastplate of righteousness, for Jesus is my righteousness. I put on the armor of light as the belt of truth, for Jesus is the truth. I put on the armor of light as the shield of faith, for Jesus is the object of my faith. I put on the armor of light as the shoes of peace, for Jesus is my peace. I put on the armor of light as the sword of the Spirit, for Jesus is the living Word.

Through the Holy Spirit, remind me of this powerful armor in times of temptation and attack. I commit myself to you as one trusting in the power and presence of Christ Jesus and not in my own strength.

THE ARMOR OF GOD

CHAPTER 7

THE ARMOR OF HOLINESS

Let us put aside the deeds of darkness and put on the armor of light.
—Romans 13:12

We have been focusing on the last part of this verse to put on the armor of light. However, we cannot ignore the first part. In fact, for the armor to be effective, we *must* put aside the deeds of darkness.

The deeds of darkness represent everything that dishonors the Lord and his Word. They represent the struggle we have as humans with sin. They represent activities that look for an alternative power source for our lives. There are many false gods that seem to promise a happy life but, in the end, bring disappointment.

Putting on the armor involves not just words, but action. The armor is not put on in a vacuum separate from our lives. The Christian life is a relationship with the Lord, and the depth of that relationship is based upon our obedience to his will. We need to create space where the Lord can work on our behalf. If we are not consciously and actively applying the grace of God to overcome sin, the armor is limited.

Romans 7 describes the Apostle Paul's struggle with the sin nature. In Galatians 5:19–21, he gives a list of the acts of the sinful nature. One is convicted when reading the list, for it all too often describes what we do. Paul gives a wonderful description of the struggle in verse 17: "The flesh desires what is contrary to the Spirit, and the Spirit what is contrary to the flesh. They are in conflict with each other, so that you are not to do whatever you want."

There is a struggle between the flesh and the Spirit for control of our lives. We have grace and the Holy Spirit as spiritual resources in order to be victorious. Through God's provision, we are more than conquerors and we can live holy lives. "He has rescued us from the dominion of darkness and brought us into the kingdom of the Son he loves" (Colossians 1:13).

> We are those who have died to sin; how can we live in it any longer? Or don't you know that all of us who were baptized into Christ Jesus were baptized into his death? We were therefore buried with him through baptism into death in order that, just as Christ was raised from the dead through the glory of the Father, we too may live a new life. (Romans 6:2–4)

It is vital to our spiritual life that we live as dead to sin and alive in Christ. There is little or no protection from attack for the person who is living in active, willful sin. Many who are struggling with constant attacks from the enemy fail to understand that it is their disobedience to the Lord that allows these attacks.

We know what truth is because we have the scriptures. Living the truth feeds our spirit and strengthens our walk. This synergistic dynamic, which is beyond the physical, results in spiritual growth.

Walking in truth eliminates false gods from our lives such as seeking after things rather than a relationship with the living Lord. It eliminates seeking for knowledge and power from non-Christian sources. The armor gives victory over and protection from occult practices, so we must not in any way compromise it.

Over and over, the scriptures teach us to put off the deeds of darkness and put on the Lord Jesus. Peter says we are to grow in the grace and knowledge of the Lord Jesus Christ and to add to our faith qualities that will make us fruitful for the Lord (2 Peter 1:3–10).

The closer we walk with the Lord, the stronger our armor. The stronger our armor, the more effective it is in our battle with sin and evil. Holy living is what makes the armor powerful and effective.

Doubt, fear, and unbelief give opportunity for the enemy to penetrate our armor and cause spiritual weakness. That is why it is so important to have strong armor. One who was a predator for the occult world has said that they could see the weakness of Christians and target them for attack. We need to put on the full armor of God so we can stand firm in times of temptation and attack. That full armor includes holy living.

There is another reason to live a life of holiness. Hebrews 1:14 says, "Are not all angels ministering spirits sent to serve those who will inherit salvation?" Angels are assigned to God's people. They are with us for our protection. As we walk in obedience to the Lord, the angelic presence is made more powerful.

For the armor to be effective, it must be accompanied by a life pleasing to the Lord. I am suggesting not perfection but a deliberate seeking after God, a desire to obey him, and the determined obedience to apply God's grace moment by moment. Spiritual armor and prayers are no substitute for the regular practice of spiritual discipline.

We are instructed over and over to deny self, take up our cross, follow Jesus, and grow in him. Here are a few examples.

- We need to renew our minds and make good choices that honor the Lord: Romans 12:2
- Overcoming evil requires love in action: Romans 12:9–21; 1 Corinthians 13
- We are to put off the old man and put on the new man: Ephesians 4; Colossians 3
- Because we have everything we need for life and godliness and because we have the precious promises of God, we are to make every effort to add Christian virtues to our faith: 2 Peter 1:3–7

The armor of light is not the only weapon against evil. Jesus quoted the scriptures when tempted in the desert and, as the above verses teach, holiness is vital to being an overcomer. Therefore, it is imperative that we read God's Word, communicate with the Lord in prayer, gather with others for worship, fast as God leads, and renew our minds, along with other spiritual disciplines. Through these practices, we grow in the grace and knowledge of the Lord Jesus. These combined practices all contribute to our victory over evil.

CHAPTER 8

TESTIMONIES

I am including some testimonies from those who have experiences with the armor of light. Remember, as with all spiritual realities, that each person is different and experiences the Lord in different ways. Your experience may not be the same as those here. Don't become discouraged if you don't "feel" anything. The armor of light is not about feelings in the physical sense but protection in the spirit realm.

"Our combined ministries subjected our family to intense spiritual warfare, and I prayed for protection every morning. One morning as I prayed, I visualized God protecting each of us. I pictured first our daughter, then our son, then Steve encircled by God's protective presence, which looked like golden light. When I prayed for myself, I was suddenly enveloped in brilliant light and profound peace. I lost all sense of time as I experienced God's Presence in this powerful way. I had not sought this experience, but I received it gratefully and was strengthened by it.

"Only two or three days later, a counseling client who was an incest survivor began remembering experiences in satanic ritual abuse …. My courageous client and I walked together into the darkness of her memories. But God had prepared me for stepping into deep darkness by first bathing me in His glorious light. I realized that experiences of

God's Presence were not only for my benefit but were also preparation for helping others." —Sarah Young, from the introduction to *Jesus Calling*

───────────────

"In my counseling practice I work with adults and married couples who struggle with fear, anger, anxiety and depression. They each walk in darkness. They don't want to walk in darkness, but some days it's hard to find a way out.

"I teach people how to put on the armor of light. I teach them to see themselves in their mind's eye as completely immersed in light as if light were covering them the same way water would cover them if they jumped into the deep end of a swimming pool. I teach them to pray peace and the light of God into every room in their house. I teach them to pray peace and light into their circumstances and peace and light into their people. I teach people to never curse darkness or circumstances or people—that gives darkness power. As you pray, see in your mind's eye, light covering rooms, circumstances and people. Light will always consume darkness. Darkness cannot avail where there is light." —Beth R., biblical counselor

───────────────

"I was in Temple University Hospital for a heart surgery. The doctors told me that I would not survive the surgery. The night before my surgery, I was alone in my room talking to God when I noticed a bright gold ball of light outside my window. It floated in my room and then floated around my head. It paused and then entered my forehead. All of my fear about death left me, and I knew that light was God. I did survive the surgery and am doing well to this day.

"I was personally abused by persons in the occult, which has made me aware of spiritual realities. I put on the armor of light as protection from those evil entities that seek to harm me. The Lord has given me a counseling ministry to persons who have experienced ritual spiritual abuse. I teach them to put on the armor of light, and their testimony is that they can actually sense the safety and security of the Lord's presence." —Kevin M., counselor

PRAYERS

It is important to commit your life to God daily and cover yourself with the armor of light. Quiet your heart before the Lord by shutting out the world around you. This can be done with worship music, quoted scripture, or silent meditation. Ask the Holy Spirit to reveal any sin for confession before moving into prayer.

Focus on the Lord and his love for you. If necessary, remind yourself of God's love for you and how you are complete in Christ. Affirm that in Jesus we have everything we need to live a godly life. It may help to picture yourself being enveloped by the presence of God as a light that covers your body and penetrates into your heart.

There is no magic in these prayers; these are given as samples and a guide. Use them as written, or write your own. Each situation may call for specialized prayer.

You can cover yourself with the armor of light, but you cannot cover someone else. These prayers reflect that. When praying for yourself, you say, "I put on the armor of light," but when praying for others, you ask God to cover them. The exception is that parents can cover their preteen children.

PRAYER FOR YOURSELF

> God, I come to you in the name of Jesus to confess that he is my Savior and Lord. I thank you that you have brought me from the darkness into the light. My spirit surrenders to the Holy Spirit as I put on the armor of light by wrapping myself in the light of your presence.

I cover my spirit, soul, and body with the glorious light of your presence. I thank you that your glory is a shield around me and that I am protected from all the power of the enemy.

Prayer at Bedtime

God my Lord, I come to you at the close of this day and praise you for giving me health and strength for my tasks. As I now enter into sleep, I cover my mind with your light, as protection from spiritual attacks of the enemy. I enter into rest believing that my spirit, soul, and body will be refreshed. Thank you for your blessing.

Prayer for Putting on the Whole Armor

God Almighty, I thank you for the provision you have made for my freedom and victory. Lord, I put on the armor of light. I cover myself with the light of your presence and glory. I put on the armor of light as the helmet of salvation, for Jesus is my salvation. I put on the armor of light as the breastplate of righteousness, for Jesus is my righteousness. I put on the armor of light as the belt of truth, for Jesus is the truth. I put on the armor of light as the shield of faith, for Jesus is the object of my faith. I put on the armor of light as the shoes of peace, for Jesus is my peace. I put on the armor of light as the sword of the Spirit, for Jesus is the living Word.

Through the Holy Spirit, remind me of this powerful armor in time of temptation and attack. I commit myself to you as one trusting in the power and presence of Christ Jesus and not in my own strength.

PRAYER FOR OTHERS

God, I come to you in the name of my Lord and Savior
Jesus Christ. As one you have translated from the
darkness to the light, my spirit surrenders to the Holy
Spirit within me. I ask you to cover _____ (insert
name or place) with the armor of light. I thank you that
the blood of Jesus and the glory of your presence will
protect _____ (insert name or place) from all the
power of the evil one.

PRAYER FOR HEALING

God, I confess that you knit me together in my mother's
womb and that I am wonderfully made. I yield my body
to you to be used as an instrument of righteousness.
Lord, my body is in need of healing, so I ask you to
cover and penetrate my body with the light of your
glory for healing. You have revealed yourself as the God
who heals, so I receive your healing presence into my
physical body. I thank you that healing is also possible
through the atonement of Jesus Christ. I thank you
for this healing power to live in physical health and
strength.

PRAYER FOR PROPERTY

Lord God Almighty, the maker of heaven and earth, I
confess Jesus Christ as my risen Lord and Savior. I thank
you for this home where I live. I am thankful that it is a
place of warmth and safety for me and my family. I now
cover this building with your light. As you set angels
with flaming swords to guard the entrance to the garden
of Eden, so surround my property with light. I ask you to
protect it from spiritual entities that seek entrance and

from physical damage from any source. I thank you for this protection.

Prayer for Spiritual Alignment

An important aspect of spiritual protection is to understand that we are, first and foremost, spiritual beings. The Bible teaches that we are spirit, soul, and body. God desires that we live from the spirit out. Therefore we need to be aligned in proper order. Here is a prayer taken in part from the book *Inspired by the Psalms* by Elizabeth A. Nixon. This should be prayed on a daily basis along with prayers for the armor of light.

> Father, I ask you to fill me with the Holy Spirit that I will be useful in your service today. Cause the gifts of the Spirit to flow through me and for the fruit of the Spirit to be manifest in my life today. I speak to my spirit, surrender to the Holy Spirit. I speak to my soul, surrender to my spirit as surrendered to the Holy Spirit. I speak to my body, surrender to my spirit as surrendered to the Holy Spirit. Further, I dedicate my body as a living sacrifice to be used in your service today.

[1]Inspired by the Psalms, Elizabeth A. Nixon Esq. Copyright 2010 While Quill Media

Questions for Reflection and Application

- In what ways are you aware of the spiritual battle in the world?

- How does it challenge you to realize that you are in a spiritual battle?

- In what way have you been personally affected by evil?

- What does it mean to live from your spirit?

- What methods have you used to protect yourself from spiritual attack?

- In what ways have you been successful in gaining victory over evil?

- Before reading this book, did you consider light to be powerful? Why or why not? What is your perspective now?

- Do you tend to pray proactively or reactively? Why?

- How do you effectively put on the full armor of God as given in Ephesians chapter 6?

- How do you effectively put on the armor of light?

- Where does your life reflect the holiness of God?

- What sins do you need to confess and repent of?

- How will you practice putting on the armor of light going forward – starting today?

About the Author

Charles A. Ness is an ordained Mennonite minister, and he has served the church for nearly fifty years. As a pastor he led two churches in spiritual renewal and numerical growth, and as an evangelist he has conducted many renewal meetings in churches and prisons across the country. For forty years he has been involved in prison ministry, and he is cofounder of Liberty Ministries. Charles has also led mission teams abroad in Central and South America and in Europe, and he and his wife, Janet, have four grown children and seven grandchildren.

Printed in the United States
By Bookmasters